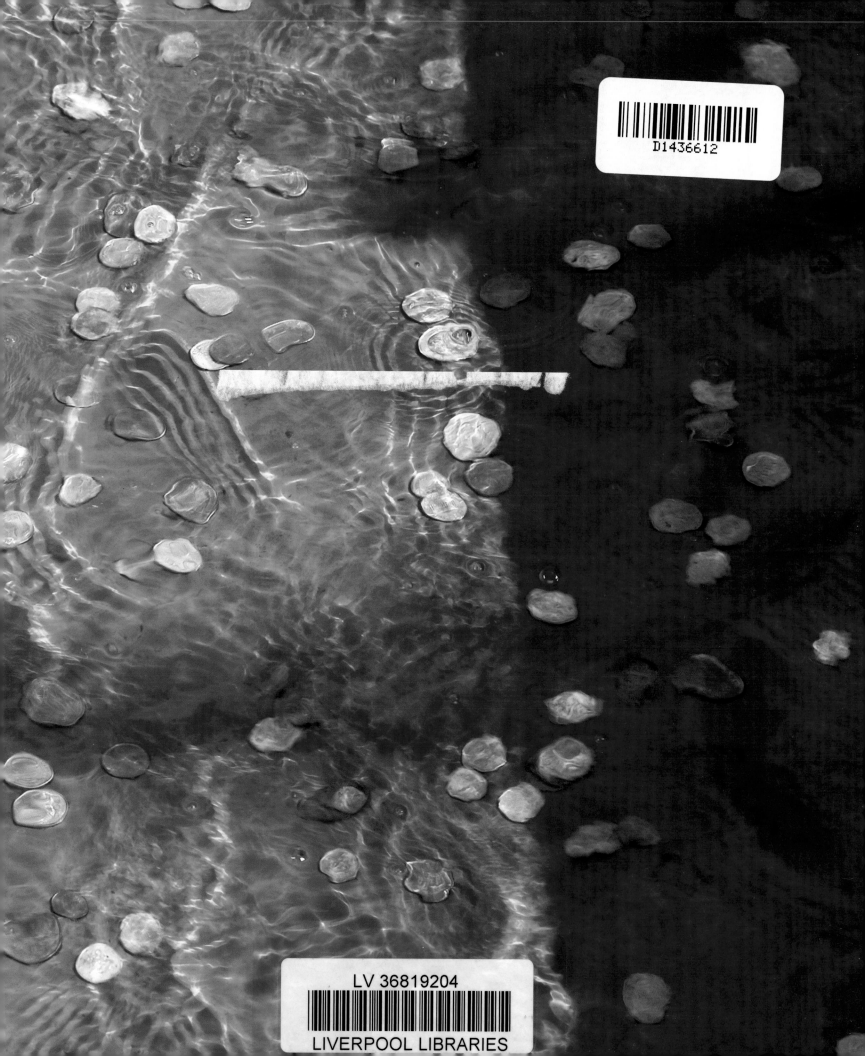

Proverbs & Sayings

For May, who did it her way

Don't put all your eggs in one basket.

Pictures to share

First published in 2013 by Pictures to Share Community Interest Company, a UK based social enterprise that publishes illustrated books for older people.

www.picturestoshare.co.uk

ISBN: 978-0-9563818-4-2

Front Cover: Two Magpies engraving from 'Little Folks' annual 1886
Endpapers: Coins in a fountain. © Harri Tahvenainen/Folio Images/Getty Images
Title page: Man with basket of eggs. © Wallace Kirkland/Time & Life Pictures/Getty Images

Proverbs & Sayings

Edited by Helen J Bate

Ne'er cast a clout till May be out

This saying first appeared in print in 1732.

The word 'clout' meant an item of clothing.

Some people think that May refers to the month of May.

Others think it refers to hawthorn blossom which is commonly known as May blossom.

May blossom usually appears at the start of May when the warmer weather comes.

Painting: Spring Walk by Timothy Easton/Bridgeman Art Library/Getty Images

Many hands make light work

This proverb dates back to the 14th century.

It explains how hard tasks can often be completed so much easier with lots of help.

The men in the picture are cleaning the glass roof of the Observatory in Kew Gardens, London, in the 1930's.

You have to kiss a lot of frogs before you find your prince.

This is a more modern popular saying.
It was inspired by the fairy tale of the
Prince who was transformed
into a frog, and back again.

It suggests that you might have to
meet a lot of unsuitable men
before you find your true love.

Painting: The Princess and the Frog by William Robert Symonds 1851 – 1934
Bradford Art Galleries and Museums/The Bridgeman Art Library/Getty Images

When the cat's away
The mice will play

This saying is believed to have
started in Roman times.

It is now often used in a
situation where a married
person is unfaithful.

Main picture: 'Pussy and I' engraving from 'Little Folks' annual 1886

You can't teach an old dog new tricks

This phrase first appeared in print in 1523 when most dogs were working animals.

Now it is often used by the elderly when young people try to teach them about new technology.

Sneeze on Monday,
sneeze for fun

Sneeze on Tuesday,
meet someone

Sneeze on Wednesday,
get a letter

Sneeze on Thursday,
get something better

Sneeze on Friday,
sneeze in sorrow

Sneeze on Saturday,
see friends tomorrow

Sneeze on Sunday,
bad luck for a week

Modern technology can now make us feel
in control of what is happening in our lives.

In years gone by superstition often provided
the explanation for things that happened.

The darkest hour is that before the dawn

This proverb was printed for the first time in 1650.

The phrase is now used to encourage optimism in times of hardship or to comfort people who are in despair.

When poverty comes in at the door, Love flies out of the window.

This saying began in medieval times.

During these times
marriage amongst the aristocracy
was sometimes more of a business arrangement.

This phrase would be used
to encourage women to stick by husbands who
had lost their fortunes.

A stitch
in time
saves nine.

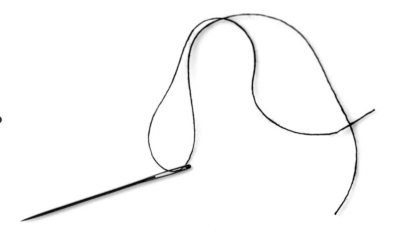

This proverb first appeared
in print in 1732.

It means that fixing
a small problem
as soon as it happens,
will stop it from getting worse.

You can lead a horse to water, But you can't make it drink

Some believe that this is the oldest truly English proverb still in use today.

It can be used nowadays to explain why the behaviour of people and organizations can be difficult to change

Photograph: Horses drinking © Volkmar Wentzel/National Geographic/Getty Images

A swarm of bees in May
Is worth a load of hay;

A swarm of bees in June
Is worth a silver spoon;

A swarm of bees in July
Isn't worth a fly.

In the Middle Ages bees were kept in
hives made of coiled and woven straw.

When the honey was harvested, the
hives and the bees were destroyed.

So every year beekepers had to find a new
swarm of bees to transfer to their new hives.

If a beekeeper was lucky enough to find a swarm
at the right time of year, he could make a lot of money.

There's a
black sheep
in every flock

This old phrase explains that in a flock
of white sheep, a black lamb is often born.

The wool from a black sheep could
not be dyed, and so was less valuable.

In English folklore, the colour black
was often associated with the devil.

The 'black sheep' came to represent
the misfit in a family.

Photograph: Shepherd with a black lamb.
© Dirk Anscutz/Taxi/Getty Images

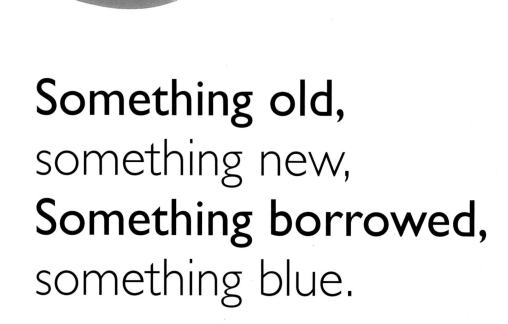

Something old,
something new,
Something borrowed,
something blue.

Superstition states that a bride should wear these four different things on her wedding day.

Wearing something blue may arise from the Roman custom of dressing brides in blue to symbolize love and purity.

It is also a superstition that a chimney sweep brings a bride and groom good luck on their wedding day

Photograph: George Harris, a chimney sweep, kisses Mrs Mary Forbat, a former Sadler's Wells opera singer. ® Bacon/Hulton Archive/Getty Images

Many things grow in the garden
that were never sown there.

This proverb was recorded for the first time in print in 1732 when the gardens of ordinary people were often full of wild flowers.

Photograph: Wild poppies against a cottage wall.
® Gary K Smith/Garden Picture Library/Getty Images

A watched pot never boils

This saying encourages people to find something else to do, while they are waiting for something good to happen.

The best-laid schemes o' mice an' men Often go awry.

This saying explains that sometimes our plans go wrong.

It comes from the poem 'To a Mouse' by Robert Burns

The poet was sad that he has destroyed the mouse's nest whilst working in the field.

Photograph: Harvest mouse in a field.
© Nature Picture Library/Britain on View/Getty Images

Mighty oaks from little acorns grow.

This well known saying originates in the 14th century.

Oak trees have always had a special status in Britain where they are seen as the kings of the forest.

But every oak tree starts life as a tiny acorn.

Main picture: Oak tree silhouette from ABC UK published by Frances Lincoln Ltd. © Helen Bate

Cold hands, warm heart.

This saying is frequently
applied to people
who seem unfriendly,
but who are really
kind and warm hearted.

As you sow,
so shall you reap

This saying originates from
the Christian Bible.

(Galatians 6:7)

It teaches the importance of goodness,
and the personal consequences
that are likely to happen
if we treat people badly.

Photograph: Boy and grandfather planting seeds.
© Dan Bigelow/The Image Bank/Getty Images

Jack of all trades, master of none.

In the Middle Ages
a 'Jack' was a labourer
who did all kinds of jobs

This saying suggests
that someone
who does lots of different jobs,
may not be very good
at any of them.

Photograph: A boy with a toy tool kit.
© Lambert/Archive Photo's/Getty Images

Birds of a feather
Flock together

This proverb goes back
to the 16th century.

It tells us that people
like to be with other people
who share the same ideas
about life.

Photograph: Flying duck ornaments on a wallpapered wall.
® Peter Dazeley/Photographer's Choice/Getty Images

If wishes were horses, then beggars would ride.

This is a 16th century proverb.

It means that if everybody could have what they wished for, then even the very poorest people would have an expensive car.

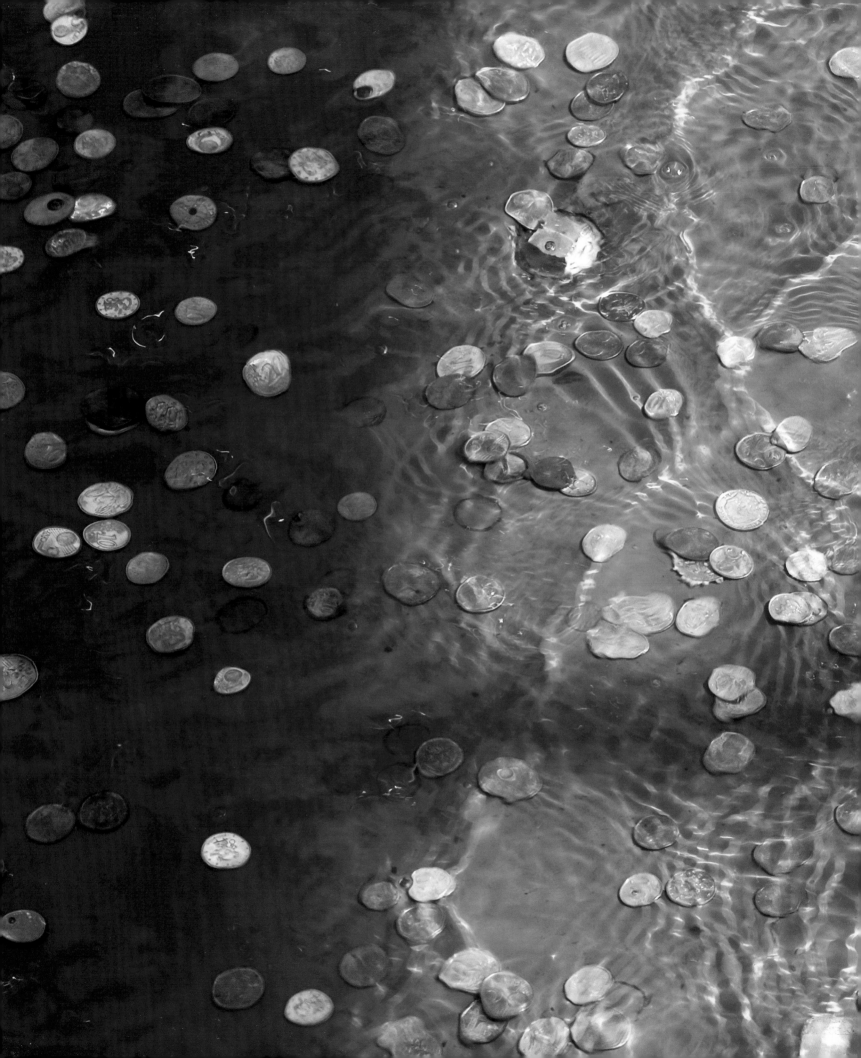